LINDSEY STIRLING

Violinist with More than 2 BILLION VIEWS

HENRIETTA TOTH

rosen publishing's
rosen central®

New York

For my niece Emi, who has taught me a lot about YouTube

Published in 2020 by The Rosen Publishing Group, Inc.
29 East 21st Street, New York, NY 10010

Library of Congress Cataloging-in-Publication Data

Names: Toth, Henrietta, author.
Title: Lindsey Stirling: Violinist with More than 2 Billion Views / Henrietta Toth.
Description: New York : Rosen Publishing Group, 2020. | Series: Top YouTube stars | Includes bibliographical references and index.
Identifiers: LCCN 2018054344 | ISBN 9781725346284 (library bound) | ISBN 9781725346277 (pbk.)
Subjects: LCSH: Stirling, Lindsey, 1986– —Juvenile literature. | Violinists—United States—Biography—Juvenile literature. | Composers—United States—Biography—Juvenile literature. | LCGFT: Biographies.
Classification: LCC ML3930.S76 T67 2020 | DDC 787.2092 [B]—dc23
LC record available at https://lccn.loc.gov/2018054344

Manufactured in the United States of America

On the cover: Dancer, violinist, and YouTube phenomenon Lindsey Stirling attends the 2015 AOL BUILD Speaker Series in New York City.

CONTENTS

INTRODUCTION 4

CHAPTER ONE
A HUMBLE CHILDHOOD 7

CHAPTER TWO
A DANCING VIOLINIST 12

CHAPTER THREE
YOUTUBE STARDOM 17

CHAPTER FOUR
RISE TO FAME 23

CHAPTER FIVE
MUSIC AND MORE 28

CHAPTER SIX
THE PERSONAL SIDE..33

TIMELINE..38
GLOSSARY 40
FOR MORE INFORMATION 41
FOR FURTHER READING..43
BIBLIOGRAPHY 44
INDEX..47

Doing two things at the same time is not an easy task. It is, however, a talent and a skill that has made American violinist and dancer Lindsey Stirling a top YouTube star. Stirling loves to play the violin and she loves to dance. So she combined her love of both into an unusual performance style as a dancing violinist.

At the beginning of her career, Stirling was not sure if a dancing violinist could be successful. While she was in college, Stirling tried playing her violin to hip-hop tracks as she danced. She performed at small clubs, parties, talent shows, and every open-mic night she could find. She knew she might be on the right career track when she played at a carnival-like neighborhood block party and saw herself billed as a hip-hop violinist.

Putting a modern twist on traditional violin playing earned Stirling the distinction of being the highest-paid female YouTube star in 2015. *Forbes* magazine listed Stirling among its 30 Under 30 in Music: The Class of 2015. During her rise to stardom, Stirling has stayed true to her unique artistic vision despite criticism from music critics. She told Samantha Sharf of *Forbes*, "The reason I succeeded is the exact reason I was told I would never succeed. I was different."

Stirling plays cover songs and also writes her own music and songs and has recorded four albums. She won a Billboard Music Award for her albums *Shatter Me* in 2015 and in 2017 for *Brave Enough*. Stirling tours the world performing in concerts and collaborates with well-known artists. She has also become a best-selling author. *The Only Pirate at the Party* is an autobiography of her childhood and her path to success. The book made the *New York Times* bestseller list in 2016. As a philanthropist, Stirling worked with the Atlanta Music Project to raise money for young people

Lindsey Stirling gives an energetic performance in Orange County, California, on April 2, 2013.

to learn about music and to perform in orchestras. In 2014, Stirling performed with Cirque du Soleil to celebrate World Water Day and to encourage water conservation.

Stirling knows that many factors have helped her become successful and also to overcome challenges. For many years, she battled the eating disorder anorexia nervosa. She has also had to cope with the illnesses and deaths of her longtime band member and friend, Jason Gaviati, and then her father, Stephen J. Stirling. Her religious faith as a member of the Church of Jesus Christ of Latter-Day Saints and the people who have come into her life have helped Stirling work through her career and personal problems. However, Stirling credits YouTube for giving her a platform for her musical performance when no one else was interested. YouTube also allowed Stirling the freedom to present her music her way. "I stumbled upon YouTube because I didn't know what else to do, and it's the best thing that ever happened to me," she told Nick Krewen of the *Toronto Star*.

CHAPTER ONE

A Humble Childhood

To learn to dance or to play the violin? That was the question in Lindsey Stirling's humble childhood. Growing up in a modest home, Stirling had to choose between two things she wanted to do. Yet, Stirling values her upbringing since it helped her to develop her artistic creativity. She made toys out of cardboard boxes and costumes from old clothes. These early skills would one day come in handy on her way to YouTube success.

Lindsey Stirling poses with her sister Brooke S. Passey at the AOL Build Speaker Series in New York City on January 12, 2016.

THE EARLY YEARS

Lindsey Stirling was born in Santa Ana, California, on September 21, 1986, to Stephen and Diane Stirling. She had an older sister named Jennifer, and two years later her younger sister Brooke was born. Lindsey also has two siblings, Marina and Vladimir, whom her parents adopted from Russia when she was in college. Lindsey was eight years old when her family moved to Gilbert, Arizona, where she grew up.

SURROUNDED BY MUSIC

Music has been a large part of Stirling's life from a very young age. Her parents liked classical music and played records at home. They also took Stirling and her siblings to concerts. "I can remember dancing around the living room with my two sisters to the music of Paganini and Mozart. I can still remember my dad combing the newspaper circling all the free concerts in town and on the weekends, we would go as a family," she recalled to Erik Kain of *Forbes*.

Stirling's desire to play violin came from watching the orchestras perform. She explained to Laurie Niles of Violinist.com, "Being exposed to so much classical music, I realized that the violin is the star of the orchestra. Today, kids see MTV—they see Taylor Swift and Katy Perry, and they want to be them. But I was exposed to violin music, and seeing that the violins have the solos, I thought, 'That's the star!'"

A DIFFICULT CHOICE

At age five, Stirling begged her parents for violin lessons. She also wanted to learn how to dance. "Ever since I was a kid, I've always wished that I could dance, but my parents said, 'You can choose violin or you can choose dance, but we can't afford both,' and I chose violin," she said in an interview with NewMediaRockstars.com. Today, dancing in her videos has fulfilled her childhood wish.

Stirling started learning to play the violin at age six using the Suzuki method of instruction. Her parents could afford only half lessons, but it was difficult to find a teacher who would give just fifteen-minute lessons once a week. Stirling practiced every day on secondhand, rented violins until she got her own instrument in the sixth grade.

SOME THINGS TO KNOW ABOUT STIRLING

Her Favorite Food Is Cereal

Stirling loves to eat cereal and has fond memories of sitting on the living room floor eating a bowl of cereal with her father.

She Loves All Things Disney

Stirling loves Disneyland and Disney characters and sometimes wishes she could live in a Disney movie. A bit of that wish came true when she competed on "Disney Night" on *Dancing with the Stars*. She danced the foxtrot to the song "When You Wish Upon a Star" from the Disney movie *Pinocchio*.

Her Favorite Television Show Is *Project Runway*

Stirling loves fashion and costume design. She pieced together odd bits of clothing and material to design the costumes for her early videos.

THE PIRATE LOOK

In the second grade, Stirling had poor reading skills. She was smart in other areas and talented on her violin, but she found reading difficult. Stirling was diagnosed with cross-dominance. It is a learning disability marked by language and scholastic difficulties and mental health issues. It means that Stirling's brain processed what she saw differently. Stirling writes in her autobiography, *The Only Pirate at the Party*, that for her cross-dominance was "a lot like dyslexia, only completely different."

The treatment included wearing an eye patch over her right eye. Stirling did not like wearing the eye patch until she imagined

Coauthor Brooke S. Passey looks on as Lindsey Stirling, with her dog, Luna, speaks during a book signing for *The Only Pirate at the Party* in Austin, Texas, on January 16, 2016.

she looked like a pirate and became interested in how pirates lived. "Pirates don't take orders or ask permission," Stirling writes in her book. "They do what they want. Allow me to clarify. If your mom asks you to do the dishes, do not pull out your pirate attitude. But if someone tells you you're not good enough, says your dreams are too lofty, or claims there is no room in showbiz for a dancing violinist—well then, by all means, pull out your eye patch, my friend, and take to the high seas."

RETHINKING THE VIOLIN

By her late teens, Stirling lost her enthusiasm for playing the violin. The strict method of instruction did not leave room for Stirling to add her personal interpretation to the classical pieces she was learning. But by playing music she was interested in listening to, such as pop tunes, Stirling learned to love the violin again. While attending Mesquite High School in Gilbert, Arizona, Stirling was in a rock band called Stomp on Melvin. She began to write her own music and develop her unique dance performance. Stirling explained to Laurie Niles of Violinist.com, "Rather than giving up on it when I started to get burned out, and I wanted to be more creative with it, to be able to create art and not just play what other people had created. So rather than switching instruments or giving up on what I had worked so hard to do, I just thought, no, I need to make the violin fit me, rather than make me fit the violin."

CHAPTER TWO

A Dancing Violinist

"Be yourself; everyone else is already taken." Stirling begins her autobiography, *The Only Pirate at the Party*, with this line from writer Oscar Wilde. Stirling realized early on that she did not have to be like everyone else to be accepted. She knew she should love herself as she was and with the talent she had.

"YOU'RE TOO DIFFERENT"

Everywhere Stirling performed she was told, "You're too different." Stirling told Morgan Jones of *Deseret News*, "I was told at first that being different was a bad thing. Everywhere I went, it was just, 'You're too different.' And it turned out that being different was the best thing that ever happened to my career. It is why people travel to my shows. It's why people want to hear my story and buy my book. The recipe for my success is that I stayed true to that." Stirling does not fit the usual stereotype of a violinist or a dancer but being different is okay with her. It has helped Stirling learn not to be bothered by criticism and rejection and still work hard.

Stirling was inspired to combine dance with violin playing by groups like Celtic Woman and Bond. Her performances were a little disorderly at first until all the parts fell into place to create her own presentation. Stirling always believed that she could succeed if she got the right breaks. She just didn't dream that it could be on such a large scale.

BEFORE YOUTUBE

Stirling's musical style started to come together when she performed during America's Junior Miss Pageant (now Distinguished Young Women Award) in 2005. She won the talent category in the state pageant with her performance of a violin rock song she wrote.

Lindsey Stirling plays her violin during the SXSW (South by Southwest) Music Festival at the Austin Music Hall in Austin, Texas, on March 15, 2014.

To launch her career, Stirling performed wherever she could get noticed. She played small gigs, like bar mitzvahs and weddings. She even played for free at some music events. When Stirling performed at a large block party, she was billed, for the first time, as a hip-hop violinist. Stirling tried to get talent agents, television shows, and record producers interested in her music but was not successful.

America's Got Talent's panel of judges, Piers Morgan (*left*), Sharon Osbourne (*second from right*), and Howie Mandel (*right*), appear along with host Nick Cannon to speak with reporters on April 15, 2011, in Pasadena, California.

ON *AMERICA'S GOT TALENT*

In 2010, Stirling was a contestant on the fifth season of the reality television show *America's Got Talent*. She was introduced as a hip-hop violinist, and she played and danced to "Tik Tok" by Kesha and "Break Your Heart" by Taio Cruz.

Seven million viewers tuned in to watch Stirling reach the quarterfinals. For Stirling, it was a moment of success. She won the audience's approval, but her performance did not sway the judges. They liked her interesting presentation yet they were not impressed by her musical skills. Judge Piers Morgan told Stirling, "You're not untalented, but you're not good enough to get away with flying through the air and trying to play the violin at the same time." Judge Sharon Osbourne said, "You need to be in a group. What you're doing is not enough to fill a theater in Vegas."

AFTER *AMERICA'S GOT TALENT*

Stirling had hoped that because *America's Got Talent* had a large audience, it would boost her career and change her life. She admitted that it was not her best performance, but she had given it her best shot. Stirling was hurt and humiliated by the judges' comments and disappointed in the show's results. "After that, the world had completely forgotten that I had existed and I went back to square zero. I kept hustling for six months and doing things like getting really low-key gigs at college campuses,

HOW TO LAUNCH A YOUTUBE CHANNEL

The popularity and influence of YouTube continues to grow. Thirty million people across the world check daily to see what's new on You-Tube. Videos can be easily filmed on a smartphone, edited on a laptop, and then uploaded to your channel.

It's simple to follow the directions on the YouTube website to start a channel. First, determine who your audience will be. For whom will you be making videos? Look at the competition and see what you can do differently. Then, produce your first video and create your channel. Give your video a title that can be easily searched on Google. Finally, set up a schedule to produce new videos and film at least one each week.

playing at noon in cafeterias," she told Nick Krewen of the *Toronto Star*. Although Stirling kept dancing and playing her violin, she also thought about quitting.

STIRLING'S FIRST VIDEO

In 2011, when Stirling's career seemed to be fizzling out, she was asked to shoot a music video by videographer Devin Graham. He produces adventure and sports videos for his YouTube channel devinsupertramp. As of early 2019, he has more than 5.3 million subscribers and more than 1 billion views.

Graham told Stirling that he thought she was talented. He wanted to make a music video of her and put it on his YouTube channel. At the time, Stirling didn't know much about YouTube and how it might help her career. Stirling's first music video was filmed against the background of a parking garage and a green park as she played her original song "Spontaneous Me." It was viewed by twenty-five thousand subscribers on Graham's channel. It kicked off Stirling's career as she gathered more views and she began filming videos for her own YouTube channel. Stirling was on her way to YouTube success, and to date, her first video has more than thirty million views.

CHAPTER THREE

YouTube Stardom

According to Stirling, life is about getting one chance after another and recognizing those chances to reach your dreams. In Stirling's case, the chance to produce albums, do concert tours, and work with music stars came in the form of YouTube.

KEY TO SUCCESS

Stirling joined YouTube in 2007. She named her channel Lindseystomp. She had uploaded a video that failed to get her on the *Ellen DeGeneres Show*. It was only after the huge response to making the video of "Spontaneous Me" with Devin Graham that Stirling saw how YouTube could be the platform for her career. "We did the video, 'Spontaneous Me,' and I was amazed. As soon as he put it up on his channel, my music, which was just sitting around on iTunes, suddenly started to sell. People were requesting more of my songs and they were loving and sharing them," Stirling told Nick Krewen of the *Toronto Star*.

In 2012, Stirling posted her breakout song and video "Crystallize" to her own YouTube channel. In it, Stirling plays the violin

Lindsey Stirling takes part in the Forbes Under 30 Summit held at the Pennsylvania Convention Center in Philadelphia on October 5, 2015.

while dancing in a palace made of ice. Within twenty-four hours, the video had one million views. Now it has more than two hundred million views.

AN ONLINE AUDIENCE

Stirling launched a traditional music career in a nontraditional way and found an audience online. In just four years, Stirling went from being unknown to being a star on YouTube and beyond. Millions of fans love her energetic and unique style of performance that includes colorful costumes. Stirling dubsteps and hip-hops her way through a variety of music. She plays her own original songs, cover songs, and her version of video game theme songs like "The Legend of Zelda."

Now, more than eleven million viewers subscribe to Lindsey Stirling (the new name of lindseystomp), making Stirling one of the highest-paid YouTubers. Her videos have been viewed more than two billion times.

The YouTube icon is easily recognized on smartphones and tablets around the world.

MAKING MUSIC VIDEOS

Even though success has happened quickly for Stirling, it has been hard work to launch and maintain her career. She is involved in every aspect of her concerts and videos from the costumes to the dance routines. Stirling makes her own videos for her channel. She learned filmmaking as a student at Brigham Young University, which, in the beginning, helped her to make professional-looking videos on a limited budget. Stirling is particularly good at editing her videos and loves piecing them together.

These days, Stirling makes an income from the ads and sponsors on her channel. Stirling says she is okay with sponsorship

PROS AND CONS OF YOUTUBE

Pros
- YouTube is a reliable platform for uploading content.
- YouTube accepts homemade and professional videos.
- Developing content for YouTube can be done inexpensively.
- YouTube offers a platform for creativity, entertainment, and education.
- YouTube reaches a large audience across the world.
- Some YouTubers make a living through their channels.

Lindsey Stirling performs in a fountain while shooting the music video for "Master of Tides" at the Americana at Brand shopping complex in Glendale, California, on August 14, 2014.

Cons
- There's pressure to produce and upload content to your channel on a schedule.
- Pressure also exists to keep the content fun and interesting for fans.
- Being a YouTube celebrity can be tiring, and some YouTubers suffer from burnout.
- Fake views of videos can inflate the real number of people watching a channel.
- Online safety is a concern, and as a result performers must avoid revealing personal information.
- Making a living as a YouTuber is not guaranteed.

as long as the promotions are not something she or her fans are ashamed of. It allows her to create her music independently.

It's hard for Stirling to choose which is her favorite video. She told the staff of *LDS Living*, "I have creatively put so much personal love and effort into all of my videos that there's a special place in my heart for all of them. I like different videos for different reasons. I think 'Roundtable Rival' is the most fun of all my videos, 'Shatter Me' carries the deepest meaning and is the most personal, and 'Shadows' is classic Lindsey—probably my most innovative creation."

AN INDEPENDENT ARTIST

Since 2012, Stirling has produced four albums. Two went gold and all came in at the top of the classical and dance charts. She has released her albums independently on her own record label Lindseystomp Records. There is no major record company involved. This has given Stirling the artistic freedom to create her music and performances without interference. Thousands of her albums have sold to a growing number of fans enthusiastic about her individual style.

Stirling has been called a classical-crossover violinist, a hip-hop violinist, a pop violinist, and even a New Age musician. But Stirling has her own idea about her style of music. "If I can only choose one category, I'd probably put it in the electronic, because the base of the music is electronic," Stirling explained to George Varga of the *San Diego Union-Tribune*. Stirling sees the violin as the lead performer in her music with the keyboards and synthesizers backing it up.

At the start of her musical career, Stirling thought she had to follow the traditional path and get a talent agent and record contract. Being unable to interest a record company in her music and then finding YouTube was really her big break. Stirling told George Varga of the *San Diego Union-Tribune*, "I just can't believe this journey my music has taken me on. My big goal was that I wanted to be someone who was pioneering the way for the independent artist with this new social media–fueled model, and show that you could cross over from YouTube and be seen as a new artist."

CHAPTER FOUR

Rise to Fame

As Stirling's online audience grew, she became popular and successful in the United States and abroad, especially in Europe. Companies started to offer Stirling and Devin Graham money to film her videos in exchange for publicity. She explained to Nick Krewen of the *Toronto Star*:

> Once we started to make a name for ourselves, people started to reach out and offer to fly me and Devin places. A travel company paid all our expenses and paid us on top of it to make a video and go to Kenya. The same thing happened in New Zealand. That was the amazing thing— once we were creating such high-quality content, we were able to fund our travels.

CONCERT TOURS

Stirling started doing concert tours in 2012. She has played sold-out events all over the world in large theaters like Humphreys Concerts by the Bay in San Diego, California, that seat 1,400 people. She has been on a two-month tour of North America and played as many as two hundred shows in two years. Sometimes Stirling is on the road for months at a time. She likes traveling with her band on a cozy tour bus and often writes music on those late-night travels from city to city. *Brave Enough*, the name of Stirling's third album and tour, took place in 2016. The tour was filmed as a documentary for the YouTube Red channel. The film looks at how personal challenges and heartbreak affected Stirling's life and concert performance.

Stirling loves to tell a story through her music and stage performance. "I love getting to transform all these songs, all these music videos, into a live performance. It's like a full emotional experience when I create a show," she told John J. Moser of the

Lindsey Stirling takes an athletic leap into the air while performing at the Bass Concert Hall in Austin, Texas, on November 7, 2016.

Morning Call. Stirling wants her audience to go on a journey with her and laugh or cry. She uses video and lighting effects and colorful costumes. Some of Stirling's dancing is athletic, so sneakers are often part of her ensemble. Stirling admits that dancing while playing the violin takes practice. She rehearses a song until she knows it well enough to dance to it.

Stirling has appeared in many different types of shows. She has played at the Kennedy Center in Washington, DC, an NBA game half-time show, and a show held in a large fountain. Stirling plays acoustic and electric violins. Her favorite instrument is an old Roth violin that has a warm sound. Her Yamaha electric violin has a clean and sharp sound. Stirling has taken violin lessons again to brush up on her skills.

STIRLING AND HER CRITICS

Some music critics have been hard on Stirling, especially at the beginning of her career. They did not like her style of performance or her music. They said it lacked boldness, emotion, and sounded like background music. They also did not know whether to label it classical or pop music. More recently, critics have noticed that Stirling has polished her performance, but some still criticize her violin playing. Stirling has been disappointed by the critics' comments, but she admits that she cannot please everyone. She also understands that classically trained violinists might not appreciate her music. But Stirling is having the last laugh because her fans are enthusiastic about her songs, videos, and concerts. They have even told her they like having her music on in the background when they are doing something else.

AWARDS AND RECOGNITION

In 2013, early in her career, Stirling won a YouTube Music Award. She shared the award with the group Pentatonix for its song "Radioactive." Stirling has been nominated for and won Billboard Music Awards. Her debut album, *Lindsey Stirling*, was nominated in 2014. In 2015, she won the Billboard Music Award for Top Dance/Electronic Album for *Shatter Me*.

At the awards ceremony, Stirling and Wiz Khalifa performed a tribute to actor Paul Walker, who died in 2013. Stirling's album *Brave Enough* won Top Dance/Electronic Album again in 2017.

In 2016, Stirling won Best YouTube Musician at the Shorty Awards, given for the best artist in social media. Her international awards include a win in Germany with an ECHO Award in 2014 for Best Crossover Act. Stirling has appeared and performed at other

Lindsey Stirling and dancer Mark Ballas are pictured at the *Dancing with the Stars* competition in Los Angeles, California, on November 6, 2017.

ceremonies, too, like the MTV Music Awards. However, she still gets uneasy walking those red-carpet events.

WORKING WITH OTHER ARTISTS

Stirling's success has given her the opportunity to collaborate with well-known musical artists. It was a special experience for Stirling to work with the group Evanescence. She had listened to them when she was in high school. Stirling appeared in concert with Andrea Bocelli at the O2 Arena in London. She filmed a video with singer John Legend, in which they perform his song "All of Me." It has more than one hundred million views. Stirling had fun filming a comical video with the Muppets and singer Josh Groban. In it, Kermit the Frog directed Groban and Stirling performing the song "Pure Imagination" from the 1971 movie *Willy Wonka and the Chocolate Factory*.

ON *DANCING WITH THE STARS*

In the fall of 2017, Stirling joined the cast of *Dancing with the Stars* for its twenty-fifth season. Stirling got to express her love of dancing and storytelling through her performances. She was paired with instructor Mark Ballas and presented different dances like the foxtrot, tango, and waltz. During the freestyle dance, Stirling played her electric violin. Stirling placed second at the end of the competition.

CHAPTER FIVE

Music and More

In addition to music, Stirling has other interests that allow her to use her talents and hobbies. She has served as a Mormon missionary, is a philanthropist, writes musical arrangements for kids, and has published a best-selling book.

MISSIONARY DAYS

The Salt Lake Temple in Salt Lake City, Utah, is the largest Mormon temple in the world.

Before Stirling became successful, she served as a missionary for the Church of Jesus Christ of Latter-Day Saints. For a year and a half, Stirling worked to teach the Gospel of Christ to people in New York City. "This was a big sacrifice, but it was so worth it," she told Jake Healey of *LDS Living*. "I had to reach down inside myself and realize that there is more to me than my desires, my style, and my hobbies. God helped me discover a new side of myself."

Stirling failed to teach anyone for the first six months of her missionary work. She felt like a failure because she had worked hard but did not see any results. Later on, Stirling did help a man to find faith. He called Stirling an angel he met on the subway. She also taught a teenage boy how to pray who did not know how.

Stirling did find time to work on her music but did not achieve any success. Yet, Stirling says that her experience in New York City was the start of her career. She learned patience and polished her social skills. The negative comments and rejection she faced during her mission helped her develop a thick skin. It also made Stirling determined to forge ahead and succeed in the music business.

A BEST-SELLING AUTHOR

Stirling can add best-selling author to her list of accomplishments. Her autobiography, *The Only Pirate at the Party*, was released on January 12, 2016. She coauthored it with her younger sister, Brooke S. Passey. Stirling writes openly about her experiences in life and in her career and how they have shaped her as a person. Stirling also gives credit to her family members and friends, who have made a difference in her life and her success. On January 31, 2016, the book made the *New York Times* best-seller list.

WRITING MUSIC

Stirling's success has encouraged young people to learn to play the violin. She advises them to practice the scales even though

THE ONLY PIRATE AT THE PARTY

Stirling's first book is a memoir of her childhood and career. Often, she would write it after an exhausting show late at night and wherever she happened to be on tour. Stirling tells funny stories about growing up and about her early days in the music business. On her first day of kindergarten, Stirling dressed herself in a kimono and a curly brown wig. When she walked the red carpet for the first time at an event, she was unprepared and wore leg warmers and an old pair of sneakers. Included are childhood snapshots and a section of photos from Stirling's concerts. Stirling makes a dedication to Jason Gaviati, her band and tour member who passed away before the book was published.

Young fans meet Lindsey Stirling during a book signing event for *The Only Pirate at the Party* in Austin, Texas, on January 16, 2016.

it might be boring and then they can play what they want. Stirling has published books of musical arrangements specifically geared for kids to follow. They include cover songs and a medley of music from stage shows like *Phantom of the Opera*. They also come with music for the piano and CDs of backtracks to accompany the violin playing. Young musicians can get sheet music of Stirling's original songs to play. Stirling has been writing original music since she was in the band Stomp on Melvin in high school. Stirling says that she writes different styles of music, but with emotions and themes. She composes in an unstructured way and just as it comes to her.

Lindsey Stirling rehearses for the Cirque du Soleil fundraising event at the Mandalay Bay Resort and Casino in Las Vegas, Nevada, on March 20, 2014.

PHILANTHROPY

Stirling helps others by taking part in humanitarian causes that are important to her. In October 2013, Stirling joined a fund-raiser for the Atlanta Music Project in Atlanta, Georgia. The organization gives children of limited opportunities the chance to experience music and perform in choirs and orchestras. Stirling remembers how important music was to her as a child and how much she wanted to learn violin. "It breaks my heart that not everybody gets that chance to have music lessons or musical instruments to play and more and more schools are cutting programs, and that's why I teamed up with the Atlantic Music Project," Stirling explained to Abby Stevens of the *Deseret News*. For the fund-raiser, Stirling provided limited-edition T-shirts with her signature and the logo the Power of Music. The money raised helped the Atlanta Music Project reach the goal of giving musical training for fifty children.

In March 2014, Stirling performed with Cirque du Soleil at a fund-raiser in Las Vegas. The Canadian entertainment company puts on an annual stage show called *One Night for One Drop*. The money raised from ticket sales helps people to have access to clean and safe water worldwide. Artists from across the entertainment industry perform in the shows, which have raised more than $25 million.

Stirling has also performed at a charity event for breast cancer and raised money to help her bandmate Jason Gaviati during his cancer treatments. She has played her violin for patients at children's hospitals. During a tour in Africa, Stirling visited Kenya. She made a video of her visit to a rural community, where she played violin at a school, played with the children, visited their homes, learned their tribal dances, and dressed in native costume. Stirling even showed a tribal member how to hold and play her violin.

The Personal Side

Music is important to Stirling, but she credits her personal life and experiences for making her who she is. Even more important than fame or success is her family and friends and her faith in God and her church.

ROLE OF FAITH IN STIRLING'S LIFE

Stirling is a Mormon, a member of the Church of Jesus Christ of Latter-Day Saints. Her religious faith and beliefs are a large part of her life. She credits God with surrounding her with amazing people who have helped her during personal challenges and throughout her musical career.

Stirling says that her career path has been directed by God. Even the results of her humiliating performance on *America's Got Talent* was part of God's plan. She told Morgan Jones of *Deseret News*, "I knew what I wanted; I was working so hard for it. I felt like I deserved it, but then I fell on my face. And that was God directing my path to a career, to a path that was so much better

Lindsey Stirling kicks her concert into high gear at the Citibank Hall in Sao Paulo, Brazil, on August 25, 2017.

for me. I can look back on my own life and see how he has directed me, and it gives me hope and clarity for my future."

ROLE OF FAITH IN STIRLING'S MUSIC

Sometimes it's a challenge for Stirling to stay true to her faith in the world of pop culture. She works with designers to keep her show costumes modest, especially the necklines and sleeves. Stirling doesn't drink alcohol and avoids parties where there is a lot of drinking. Even when she's on a concert tour, Stirling tries to go to church.

Stirling has turned down offers to work with some well-known artists because their music or videos were crude and went against her moral standards. That was especially hard to do in the early days of Stirling's career when she would have liked the professional exposure.

CHALLENGES IN LIFE

Stirling's personal life has been affected by what she says was a "dark" time. In November 2015, her best friend and the keyboard player in her band, Jason "Gavi" Gaviati, died of cancer. He had played with Stirling since her very first concert tour. Soon after Gavi's death, Stirling's father, Stephen J. Stirling, was diagnosed with cancer. Her father passed away in January 2017. "Sometimes when you least expect it, life changes and life hits you," Stirling said to Morgan Jones of *Deseret News*. "I just had some things that I went through that really reminded me that none of this matters—no money, no amount of fame. What's important is the people around me." To get through these difficult times, Stirling relied on her religious faith. She read passages in scripture about the afterlife that teach about one day seeing again those loved ones who have passed on.

Losing two important people in her life had a strong impact on Stirling's music. The songs she wrote at the time were dark and depressing. They did not have any real depth, and Stirling realized that to write about her emotions she had to deal with them first. She shared these emotions in her 2016 album *Brave Enough*.

A HEALTH BATTLE

In her early twenties, Stirling struggled with the eating disorder anorexia nervosa. She also suffered from depression. Stirling's choices about how to eat or not to eat took over her life. Eventually, she realized that it also made her very unhappy. Publicly admitting that she had anorexia and using it in her music helped Stirling to work through her health battle.

ANOREXIA NERVOSA

Anorexia nervosa is a type of eating disorder. It is quite common and more than two hundred thousand cases are diagnosed in the United States each year. More girls and women struggle with it than men. Well-known people who have had eating disorders include Hilary Duff, Kesha, and Demi Lovato.

Symptoms of anorexia include body weight that is abnormally low. Anorexics are obsessive about how much they weigh and what and how much they eat. They might exercise too much to stay too thin. Treatment includes counseling and therapy. Hospitalization is sometimes required for anorexics to regain their normal body weight. If not treated, serious complications of anorexia include malnutrition and organ failure.

Singer Demi Lovato, who struggles with an eating disorder, is photographed at the American Music Awards in Los Angeles, California, on November 19, 2017.

Stirling's song "Shatter Me," from her album of the same name, is about her struggles with anorexia. She also tells her story in the video for the song. "It's symbolic of feeling trapped in an emotional box. Which is what I once had—I once had anorexia, and 'Shatter Me' is all about this ballerina and this music box, which represents me being stuck inside this mental disease and wanting to break free and crying out for help and finally having the courage to break free," she told John J. Moser of the *Morning Call*.

LOOKING TO THE FUTURE

Stirling has become successful in the music world by forging her own path. She continues to think outside the box and is not afraid to try new things. As actress Lucille Ball, one of Stirling's idols, said, "I'd rather regret the things I've done than regret the things I haven't done." In the coming years, Stirling would like to tour less and have a family someday. She dreams of having a show on Broadway and in Las Vegas. It would give her a permanent base to raise a family so she could continue to write music and perform it her way.

TIMELINE

1986 Stirling is born on September 21.

2002 Stirling joins the rock band Stomp on Melvin.

2007 On May 20, Stirling launches her YouTube channel, lindseystomp.

2010 On April 27, Stirling is a quarterfinalist on *America's Got Talent*.

2011 Stirling releases her first music video for her song "Spontaneous Me" on May 18.

2012 Stirling releases the music video for her song "Crystallize." It becomes the eighth-most-viewed video on YouTube with more than one hundred million views. Stirling's debut album, *Lindsey Stirling*, is released on September 18. On September 22, Stirling begins her first world concert tour.

2013 On January 25, Stirling admits to battling anorexia nervosa. On October 1, Stirling joins with the Atlanta Music Project to bring music appreciation to children. Stirling performs on the talk show *Conan* on October 24. Stirling and the group Pentatonix win a YouTube award for their version of the song "Radioactive" on November 3.

2014 Stirling releases her second album, *Shatter Me*. It posts at number two on the Billboard pop album chart. Stirling performs with Cirque du Soleil to celebrate World Water Day on March 22. Stirling kicks off her second world tour on May 13. Stirling is nominated for a Teen Choice Award.

2015 Lindseystomp reaches six million subscribers on January 19. Stirling wins Artist of the Year in the YouTube Awards on March 23. *Shatter Me* wins Top Dance/Electronic Album at the Billboard Music Awards on May 17. In August, Stirling graduates from Brigham Young University.

2016 Stirling's autobiography, *The Only Pirate at the Party*, is released on January 12. On January 31, the hardcover makes the best-seller list for nonfiction. Stirling releases her third album, *Brave Enough*, on August 19. Stirling begins her third concert tour.

2017 *Brave Enough* wins Top Dance/Electronic Album at the Billboard Music Awards on May 21. The YouTube documentary about Stirling, *Brave Enough*, debuts on September 5. On October 20, Stirling releases her fourth album, *Warmer in the Winter*. Stirling finishes second on *Dancing with the Stars* on November 21.

2018 Stirling appears at the Alaska State Fair on September 3. Stirling begins The Wanderland Tour on November 23 to mark the rerelease of her 2017 holiday album *Warmer in the Winter*.

GLOSSARY

anorexia nervosa An eating disorder marked by obsessive thoughts about weight and diet.

autobiography A person's life story written by that person.

backtracks Recorded music that is played along with a live musical performance.

choreography The arrangement of steps or moves for a performance.

cover song A recording or performance of a song by someone other than the original artist.

cross-dominance A learning disability marked by how the brain processes information.

debut The first appearance of a product.

dubstep A type of electronic dance music that emerged in the late 1990s.

dyslexia A learning disorder that makes it hard to read or understand written words.

gospel A religious teaching or belief.

kimono A robe-like garment originally worn in Japan.

memoir The story of someone's emotions and memories.

missionary A person who goes on a mission to promote a religion through education and service.

Mormon A person belonging to the Church of Jesus Christ of Latter-Day Saints.

open-mic An event where nonprofessional entertainers can perform.

philanthropy The donation or raising of money for a worthy cause.

platform A space to bring attention to one's work through social media and other ways.

scales (musical) A set order of musical notes according to pitch.

Scripture The books of the Bible.

stereotype A belief or an idea about a person, thing, or place.

FOR MORE INFORMATION

IMDB (Lindsey Stirling's page)
Website: https://www.imdb
.com/name/nm4826530
Stirling's page on the movie,
television, and video online
database IMDB has trivia,
quotes, photos, and information on her appearances.

Lindsey Stirling
Website: https://www.youtube
.com/user/lindseystomp
Stirling's YouTube channel has
music videos, collaborations
with other artists, videos
from concert tours, and the
documentary *Brave Enough*.

Lindsey Stirling Official Website
Website: http://www
.lindseystirling.com
Facebook: @lindseystirlingmusic
Twitter and Instagram:
@lindseystirling
YouTube: Lindsey Stirling
Stirling's website lists her
upcoming tour dates and
where to buy her music. It
also includes links to photos,

videos, and other information.

LindseyTime
Website: https://www.youtube
.com//user/LindseyTime
This YouTube channel has more
personal uploads,
like Stirling's skin care secret
and behind-the-scenes videos.

**Smithsonian National Museum
of American History**
Constitution Avenue NW
Between 12th and 14th Streets
Washington, DC 20560
(202) 633-1000
Website: http://americanhistory
.si.edu
Facebook: @americanhistory
Twitter: @amhistorymuseum
YouTube: National Museum of
American History
The shirt worn by Lindsey Stir-
ling in her breakout video
"Crystallize" is in the collec-
tion of this museum.

YouTube

901 Cherry Avenue
San Bruno, CA
(650) 253-0000
Website: https://www.youtube
.com
Facebook, Twitter, and
Instagram: @YouTube
YouTube is a video-sharing
website founded in 2005. It
is now part of Google.

Violin Lab

Email: violinlab@gmail.com
Website: http://violinlab.com
Teach yourself the violin
through online videos
offered here.

FOR FURTHER READING

DK. *Video Ideas: Full of Awesome Ideas to Try Out Your Video-Making Skills*. London, UK: DK Children, 2018.

Furgang, Adam. *20 Great Career-Building Activities Using YouTube*. New York, NY: Rosen Publishing, 2017.

Hall, Kevin. *Creating and Building Your Own YouTube Channel*. New York, NY: Rosen Publishing, 2017.

Juilly, Brett. *Make Your Own Amazing YouTube Videos: Learn to Film, Edit, and Upload Quality Videos to YouTube*. New York, NY: Racehorse for Young Readers, 2017.

McAneney, Caitie. *Online Safety: Let's Talk About It*. New York, NY: Rosen Publishing, 2015.

Stirling, Lindsey. *Lindsey Stirling Favorites: Violin Play-Along*. Milwaukee, WI: Hal Leonard, 2016.

Stirling, Lindsey, and Brooke S. Passey. *The Only Pirate at the Party*. New York, NY: Gallery Books, 2016.

Tashjian, Janet, and Jake Tashjian. *My Life as a YouTuber*. New York, NY: Henry Holt and Co., 2018.

Willoughby, Nick. *Digital Filmmaking for Kids*. Hoboken, NJ: John Wiley & Sons, 2015.

Willoughby, Nick. *Making YouTube Videos: Star in Your Own Video*. Hoboken, NJ: John Wiley & Sons, 2016.

BIBLIOGRAPHY

Admin. "Lindsey Stirling Talks Competing on DanceOn's 'Dance Showdown' Season 3, New Album." NewMediaRockstars .com, October 30, 2013. http://newmediarockstars .com/2013/10/lindsey-stirling-talks-competing-on -danceons-dance-showdown-season-3-new-album -interview.

Collins, Simon. "Classical Crossover Queen Silences Critics." *Western Australian*, April 4, 2017. https://www.google .com/amp/s/thewest.com.au/entertainment/classical -crossover-queen-silences-critics-ng-b88423583z.amp.

Cutforth, Dan, and Jane Lipsitz. *Brave Enough*. Magical Elves Productions and YouTube Red, 2017.

DeMers, Jayson. "7 Reasons to Start a YouTube Channel Now (and the First Steps to Take)." *Forbes*, May 30, 2018. https:// www.forbes.com/sites/jaysondemers/2018/05/30/7-reasons -to-start-a-youtube-channel-now-and-first-steps-to take.

Fairley, James Dean. "The Pros and Cons of YouTube Business Marketing." LinkedIn, March 31, 2015. https://www.linkedin .com/pulse/pros-cons-youtube-business-marketing-james -dean-fairley.

Healey, Jake. "5 Famous Mormons Who Served Missions (& Where)." *LDS Living*, July 16, 2015. https://ldsmissionaries .com/5-famous-mormons-who-served-missions-where.

Jones, Morgan. "Dancing Violinist Lindsey Stirling Discusses Her New Book, LDS Faith and Taking a Different Route to Stardom." *Deseret News*, January 15, 2016. https://www .deseretnews.com/article/865645484/Dancing-violinist -Lindsey-Stirling-discusses her-new-book-LDS-faith-and -taking-an-untraditional.html.

Kain, Erik. "The Dancing Violinist: How Lindsey Stirling Is Conquering YouTube One Video At a Time." *Forbes*, August 29, 2012. https://www.forbes.com/sites/erikkain/2012/08/29/the-dancing-violinist-how-lindsey-stirling-is-conquering-youtube-one-video-at-a-time/#6993ad633baa.

Keller, Michael H. "The Flourishing Business of Fake YouTube Views." *New York Times*, August 11, 2018. https://www.nytimes.com/interactive/2018/08/11/technology/youtube-fake-view-sellers.html.

Krewen, Nick. "Violinist Lindsey Stirling Credits YouTube with Meteoric Rise." *Toronto Star*, June 13, 2014. https://www.thestar.com/entertainment/music/2014/06/13/violinist_lindsey_stirling_credits_youtube_with_meteoric_rise.html.

LDS Living staff. "Lindsey Stirling Passed Up Collaboration with Big Stars Because of Her Standards." *LDS Living*, April 2013. http://www.ldsliving.com/Lindsey-Stirling-Passed-Up-Collaboration-with-Big-Stars-Because-of-Her-Standards/s/81863.

Moser, John J. "Fiddling with Convention: Dancing violin virtuoso Lindsey Stirling, coming to Sands, is high octane, joyous and hip." *Morning Call*, July 27, 2018. http://www.mcall.com/entertainment/lehigh-valley-music/mc-ent-lindsey-stirling-interview-sands-bethlehem-20180720-story.html.

Niles, Laurie. "Violinist.com Interview with Lindsey Stirling: The Scene in the Song." Violinist.com, October 1, 2014. https://www.violinist.com/blog/laurie/201410/16239.

Philipkoski, Kristen. "Why Not Winning America's Got Talent and Avoiding a Major Record Label Was Awesome for Lindsey Stirling." *Forbes*, August 31, 2015. https://www.forbes.com/sites/kristenphilipkoski/2015/08/31/hy-not-winning-americas-got-talent-and-avoiding-a-major-record-label-was-awesome-for-lindsey-stirling/#5ec7da0c73a5.

Sharf, Samantha. "The 11 Best Pieces Of Advice For All Millennials From The Under 30 Summit." *Forbes*, October 7, 2015. https://www.forbes.com/sites/samanthasharf/2015/10/07 /the-11-best-pieces-of-advices-for-all-millennials-at-the-under -30-summit/#2e9862636c38.

Stevens, Abby. "Violinist Lindsey Stirling Backs Power of Music Fundraiser." *Deseret News*, October 3, 2013. https://www .deseretnews.com/article/865587591/Violinist-Lindsey -Stirling-backs-Power-of-Music-fundraiser.html.

Stirling, Lindsey, and Brooke S. Passey. *The Only Pirate at the Party*. New York: Gallery Books, 2016.

Templeton, David. "Lindsey Stirling on her 'Brave' New Album and the Power of Practice." *Strings*, August 25, 2016. http:// stringsmagazine.com/lindsey-stirling-on-her-brave-New -album-and-the-power-of-practice.

Varga, George. "Lindsey Stirling Bows Way to the Top." *San Diego Union-Tribune*, May 13, 2014. https://www .sandiegouniontribune.com/entertainment/music/sdut -lindsey-stirling-interview-2014may13-htmlstory.html.

INDEX

A

albums, 4, 17, 21, 22, 26
  Brave Enough, 4,
    24–25, 26, 35
  Lindsey Stirling, 26
  Shatter Me, 4, 26, 37
America's Got Talent,
  14–15, 33
anorexia nervosa, 6, 35,
  36, 37
awards, 26–27
  Billboard Music
    Award, 4, 26
  ECHO Award, 26
  Shorty Awards, 26

C

childhood, 6, 8
Church of Jesus Christ
  of Latter-Day Saints,
  6, 28–29, 33
Cirque du Soleil, 6, 32
collaborations, 4, 27
concert tours, 4, 19,
  23–24
costumes, 9, 19, 25
cover songs, 4, 19
critics, 4, 14–15, 25
cross-dominance, 10

D

dancing violinist, 4, 9,
11, 13, 17–18, 25, 27
Dancing with the Stars,
  9, 27

F

Forbes 30 Under 30 in
  Music, 4

G

Gaviati, Jason, 6, 30,
  32, 35
Graham, Devin, 16, 17,
  23

H

hip-hop, 4, 13, 14, 19, 22

I

income, 4, 19, 21
interesting facts, 9, 25

L

Lindseystomp Records,
  22–23

O

*Only Pirate at the Party,
  The*, 4, 10, 12, 28,
  29, 30
  name inspiration,
    9–10
New York Times

best-seller, 4, 29
original songs, 4, 11,
  17, 19, 31, 35, 37

P

Passey, Brooke S., 8, 29
philanthropy, 4, 6, 28, 32

S

siblings, 8
Stirling, Diane, 8
Stirling, Stephen J., 6,
  8, 35
Stomp on Melvin, 11, 31

V

violin, 8–9, 11, 29, 31
  Suzuki method, 9, 11

Y

YouTube, 4, 6, 15, 16,
  17, 18, 20, 21, 22
  Lindseystomp/
    Lindsey Stirling,
    17, 19
  Music Award, 26
  success, 4, 6, 7, 16,
    17, 18–19, 22

ABOUT THE AUTHOR

Henrietta Toth has written several nonfiction books for children. She is an editor with twenty years of experience in academic publishing. She has learned a lot by working on books about many different topics. Now she has learned a lot about YouTube, but she is still just learning to play her violin.

PHOTO CREDITS